Newport

IN OLD PHOTOGRAPHS

King Alphonse of Spain, who married Princess Ena, daughter of Princess Beatrice and granddaughter of Queen Victoria. The king often stayed in Newport and is seen here after winning a cup in a shooting contest in 1912.

Newport

IN OLD PHOTOGRAPHS

DONALD A. PARR

Alan Sutton Publishing Limited
Phoenix Mill · Far Thrupp · Stroud
Gloucestershire

First Published 1994

Copyright © Donald A. Parr, 1994

Cover photograph: The High Street, looking
towards the Guildhall, early 1900s.

British Library Cataloguing in Publication Data.
A catalogue record for this book is available from
the British Library.

ISBN 0-7509-0760-6

Typeset in 9/10 Sabon.
Typesetting and origination by
Alan Sutton Publishing Limited.
Printed in Great Britain by
Ebenezer Baylis, Worcester.

Contents

	Introduction	7
1.	The People	9
2.	Harbour and Estuary	41
3.	One Hundred Years of Transport	51
4.	Shops	69
5.	Around the Town	85
6.	Parades and Celebrations	113
7.	Porchfield	121
	Acknowledgements	128

Alexander Green. Known as 'Holy Joe', he lived in a cave at Ventnor and travelled around preaching and distributing tracts, existing on food given to him. He is seen here in Newport, early 1900s.

St James Square, 1890s. The weekly cattle and sheep market was held here, and the animals' drinking trough is where the Victoria monument now stands.

Introduction

After consulting many of those interested in the preservation of the island's history, it was decided to record the last hundred years or so of photography in five separate books covering the areas of Newport, Ryde, Cowes and East Cowes, the South Wight and the West Wight.

While compiling this first volume I experienced a great deal of pleasure, not only in nostalgic memories of friends and colleagues long since departed, but also in the Newport of yesteryear: the buses in The Square prior to the advent of the bus station in South Street and the old shops, some sadly no longer with us. Who among the older residents of Newport can forget a 'Larby's lardy cake' or a train ride to Cowes and other parts of the Isle of Wight?

With progress comes new enterprises and for each generation a new past. One of the aims of the 'Britain in Old Photographs' series is to preserve the old pictures which appear in family albums and collections and, in this case, create a pictorial record of Newport to record the changes in the buildings, the countryside and the people themselves.

As an island we are a small community with a strong sense of history. Many archivists have retained photographic records and most of them have been eager to cooperate with this project which is, after all, an exercise in preserving our heritage for posterity.

Like most places, Newport has altered considerably, for better or for worse. I do hope that some of the photographs used in this volume will allow the present generation of residents as well as visitors to see Newport as it was from the mid-1800s to the mid-1900s, and to see how it differs from today. I have endeavoured to name as many people as possible who appear in these photographs, but I have not always been successful. However, I hope that many older residents will recognize a friend or relative.

One change for the better is the lack of flooding around Coppins Bridge, now with its large roundabout. In days gone by floodwater would spread from the River Medina, turning the lower High Street into a lake. On the other hand, there was the thrill as a small child of seeing the quay busy with coal barges and boats, lined up ready to discharge their cargoes, or the smell and noise of the steam engines, which to the bystander held far more fascination than would the unloading of a present-day diesel lorry.

As with many towns, Newport has spread beyond its original boundaries and one of the biggest problems is planning. Everyone with an inch of ground seems to want to build something on it. Let us hope that the planners stand firm in preserving the town of Newport as much as possible.

SECTION ONE

The People

Tom Carter, known locally as 'Farmer Tom', sits in his horse-drawn bath chair. The chair belonged to Queen Victoria. It was given to him after her death in 1901, by a member of the staff at Osborne House. He then adapted it for use with his horse.

This much loved character, seen here in 1890, was deaf and dumb. Because of his disability he was known as 'Dummy', a nickname acceptable at that time.

Mr Linnington, market superintendent, is shown collecting market tolls, one of his many tasks, August 1927.

Mrs Hall, wife of Capt. Douglas B. Hall, the Tory candidate, is seen on the hustings during the election of 1909. Hall won the seat and became MP for the island.

William Rolf. William was one of the Rolf brothers who worked at his father's haulage business in Chapel Street. He is seen here in the 1930s.

Mr Chiverton, the one-legged cycle dealer, seen here in the 1920s. He modified his tricycle by adding a hand crank to help him up hills. Note the acetylene lamp; these were not often used for bicycles.

A motor cycle and side-car of the 1920s. Although the passenger is not known she must certainly have had difficulty with her floral hat! The side-car is made from wickerwork.

Wilfred Barton drives his Rolls-Royce taxi in Castle Road, 1920s.

Frank Prince, the blacksmith, owned a forge in Sea Street with his sons Frank and Harry. He is believed to have been the last man in the area to make ox shoes, which he produced between 1920 and 1922.

Walking advertisements for Atora Suet visit the forge, early 1920s. The oxen are being shod by Frank Prince (bending) and Dick Olds, as the patient driver holds the beasts. The oxen were specimens bred solely for advertising and show purposes.

The interior of the forge. Pictured, left to right: Frank Prince, Dick Olds, Harry Prince.

A Sunday School outing, believed to be from the Victoria Methodist Church in Pyle Street, 1912.

One of the early horse-drawn milk floats from the Isle of Wight Creameries, with milkman Reg Hannam and his son John, 1942.

This cobblers' workshop was situated in Carisbrooke High Street. Seen here is the owner, Mr Coward, who ran a weekly delivery service from the 1900s.

Barton Infants' School, 1907.

A group from Barton School parades at Snooks Hill in the 1890s. Pupils were then known as 'Boneheads', a nickname which has stuck until the present day.

Another group of Barton 'Boneheads' pose in the school playground, 1930s. The class is believed to be Standard 4, and included Peter Meech, Stanley Piner, Arthur Calvert, J. Crowe, Jack Wheeler and 'Darby' Hookey.

The Barton School choir, late 1940s. The teachers are 'Knobby' Clark (front right) and Tom (Bill) Boyland.

The next five photographs are all of the Newport Grammar School, believed to have been taken in 1937. Unfortunately we are unable to name all of the pupils. Can you spot a friend?

This group includes Drudge, Moore, Clark, Gaunt, White, Cawley, Flux and Wray.

The teachers pictured above and below include Miss Bright (French), Mr Richards (Maths), Mr Carr (?), Revd Mr Wheatley (headmaster) and Mr Florence (Art).

This group includes A. White, ? Marshall, ? Ramage, ? Powell, ? Conlon, ? Dabell, ? Richards, ? Pocock, ? Day, ? Turner and J. Wheatley.

Included here are the Harvey brothers, Eric Morris (a prefect), ? Webb, ? Wheatley and Ray Price.

A group from Node Hill Infants' School, with their teacher, Miss Plumb, 1930s.

At the end of the Second World War many Victory in Europe street parties took place. This one was at Hillside.

Each Christmas during the 1930s the Royal British Legion held a children's party in the Queens Hall. This photograph shows the party of 1930.

The only information we have about this photograph is that it shows a group from Parkhurst Girls' School. Are you in it?

Parkhurst Girls' School. Is this the netball team?

Newport Ladies Hockey Team, 1940. The group includes Dorothy Stevens (dark jersey), Constance Gray and Thelma Baker (front row, centre). All were members of the Victoria Sports Club.

The staff of Newport post office, 1910, pictured in what is now Lugley Street car park.

The Cement Mills Football Club 1st Eleven, 1936/7 season.

The Newport Football Club 2nd Eleven, 1922/3 season.

Newport Trojans Sports Club, pictured at Church Litton. The date is unknown.

The wool fair, 1910. This was held annually at The Rink, off Lugley Street, and fleeces were auctioned there.

The Newport Home Guard, 1944.

The Southern Vectis Bus Co. Home Guard Unit, *c.* 1943.

Newport Fire Brigade pose outside the Guildhall Fire Station with trophies gained for the inter-brigade competition, 1929.

In 1940 the fire station was placed on a war footing and presented with a mobile canteen.

A full parade and inspection took place after the presentation of the mobile canteen. It is interesting to note that the station in 1940 was only a single-storey building. The upper storey was added in January 1960.

Firemen tackle a blaze at Sherratts' electrical shop in the High Street, 26 May 1962.

While dealing with the blaze fireman Alf Phillips rescues a small child, watched by ambulance driver Charlie Harvey. I am pleased to say that the child was unhurt.

Newport Salvation Army Band, 1951. Included here are Ray Lindsay, Ron Drayton, Brian Mills, Ray Pragnall, Bob Kelly, Mr Clarke, Mr Pragnall sen., Bill West and Albert Colebrook.

The Freshwater Red Cross float at Newport Carnival. Standing by the float (left) is Miss Life, known as 'Lifey'.

Ted Fairweather, a postman, is the Newport Pearly King, seen here in the 1930s.

Nesta Meech ran her own concert group, which was famous for Christmas pantomimes.

An eyecatching float at the Newport Carnival, mid-1950s.

A Nesta Meech concert party entertains troops at the Queen's Hall during the war. Nesta is seated in the centre (left); the party also includes Bill Ward, Ted Fairweather, Jean Redstone, Pete Raynor and Miss Croft.

Carisbrooke Church choir, 1930s. Third from the right is Les Rodaway, a reporter for the *Isle of Wight County Press*.

Corporal White. In 1929 he was on escort duty, taking a deserter to Catterick in Yorkshire. While on the train the deserter murdered him. White's body was returned to the Isle of Wight and he was given a full military funeral at Newport in May of that year.

The funeral procession of Corporal White passes along Fairlee Road.

Mr Quinton, a builder and undertaker, leads a horse-drawn hearse in The Mall in the early part of the century.

Ladies of the Royal British Legion on route to a rally at Carisbrooke Castle, 1920s. The standard bearer is Miss Philpott.

At the same rally, ladies parade at the castle.

A pageant at Carisbrooke Castle, 1907.

Queen Mary and Princess Beatrice at Carisbrooke Castle, 1937.

The Princess Beatrice organ is seen here being played by Mr Abraham, organist at Carisbrooke, as PC Whillier looks on, 1937. The organ was given to the princess by the people of the island and is now kept in Carisbrooke Castle Museum.

Queen Victoria receives an illuminated address from the Mayor of Newport, James George jun., 1887.

Princess Beatrice and the Bishop of Winchester leave St Thomas' Church after the first armistice service to be held on the island, 1920s.

The Queen signs the visitors' book, watched by Alderman Drudge, Mayor of Newport, 1965.

SECTION TWO

Harbour and Estuary

MV *Wight*, Mew Langton's first vessel. Note the open wheelhouse.

A view of Newport Harbour, looking south, 1904. It is interesting to see the large amount of open quay space available for the unloading of cargo.

The inner harbour, 1920. The building on the right is now The Quay Arts Centre and buildings in the background are now waterside houses.

A view of Newport Harbour, showing the railway viaduct, 1904.

This view of the harbour made a popular postcard in 1904. The building with the large chimney (left) is the old Newport gasworks.

Mr and Mrs Leigh are pictured at the helm of their barge *Gazelle*, early 1920s.

A barge unloads its cargo at the inner harbour quay, 1902.

As well as serving Newport Harbour the River Medina was used to run water-mills. Many tributaries ran from the mill ponds into the river, and seen here is Lukely stream in full flood following a cloud burst, 1960.

Shide Path is under water during the same floods, October 1960.

The River Medina is seen here in flood at the Barley Mow public house, Shide, 1960.

Flooding at Coppins Bridge.

This photograph shows the River Medina in flood at Pan Bridge, October 1960.

The 1960 floods were some of the worst on record, and the river burst its banks in more than one place: (above) East Street; (below) the lower High Street.

Another view of the Barley Mow at Shide during the 1960 flood. The old station house is in the background (centre).

The River Medina is seen here covered in ice, winter 1963.

Ice floes on the River Medina create an impressive scene.

SECTION THREE

One Hundred Years
of Transport

A four-in-hand donkey cart stands in the yard of The Plough at Node Hill, 1889.

St James Square. It is shown (above) in the 1920s and (below) in the 1950s. Note how little room is left for other traffic to pass.

An old Enterprise bus is pictured in the early 1920s, and carries an advertisement for Athletic Motor Sports held at Newport Recreation Ground.

One of the first Vectis buses, early 1930s.

A children's charabanc outing. It was unusual to have side screens: maybe these were used to keep the children in?

A works' outing from Fred Trim's, wholesale fruit and vegetable merchants in Lugley Street, 1932. First on the left is the driver, Reg Davies.

A Golden Rod coach, *c.* 1919. Leaning on the bonnet is the driver, Jack Wavell, who lived to be ninety-three.

Members of Albany Rovers Football Club are seen here in a type of charabanc nicknamed 'The Toast Rack'. The location is St James Square, 1920.

A group of Newport residents take a charabanc to Brighton, *c.* 1920.

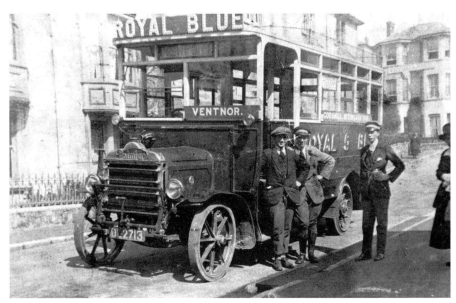

A Royal Blue Bus on route from Newport to Ventnor, 1923.

After driving for Golden Rod coaches, Jack Wavell joined Enterprise Buses in the early 1920s. Sitting inside are Mr Wavell sen. and his granddaughter.

J. Seely MP (later the 1st Lord Mattistone) opens a new drinking-fountain in St James Square, 1905. Note the Royal Navy recruitment poster on the wall (right).

Holyrood Street, 1900s. A haulier with his horse and cart returns to the railway station.

The entrance to Newport railway station, 1955. It was closed in 1966 and was demolished to make way for an industrial estate.

A Southern Vectis lorry, *c.* 1930.

Newport's first motorized fire engine. It is a 1920 Model T Ford, with bodywork and pumps by Stanley. It was kept with a Model T ambulance at the Guildhall Fire Station, until it was scrapped in 1941.

A delivery lorry, belonging to corn merchants John Sheath & Co., *c*. 1920. The driver is Mr Pointer.

An earlier form of transport arrives at Shide Cross, 1899.

On the opening of the Royal Hotel at Sandown, 1936. Wray & Sons of Newport were commissioned to regularly supply the hotel with groceries. All their vans were required for the journey and they lined up in convoy outside their shop.

Mockford & Chandler were cycle dealers and, like many in their day, they also charged accumulators and sold a wireless set or two. Taken in the 1930s, this photograph shows Mr Mockford (left) and Mr Chandler (right).

One of the problems facing builders of the early railways on the island was how to pass the lines through the town of Newport. Two main areas were affected: the river at Coppins Bridge and the Lukely stream at Hunnyhill. The problem was overcome by the construction of viaducts spanning not only the river, to avoid the risk of flooding, but also the road. This photograph shows the original iron viaduct at Coppins Bridge.

A train pulls in to Newport station, early 1920s.

The view from a train as it is about to cross the River Medina.

A train crosses the viaduct over the Lukely stream at Hunnyhill.

A Crouchers steam lorry stands outside their depository in Quay Street. The lorry is a Clayton and Shuttleworth. It has solid iron wheels and dates from *c.* 1910. The trailer is a converted horse-drawn pantechnicon, and a draw bar has replaced the shafts.

Two tank engines stand at the centre platforms of Newport railway station, early 1950s.

Carisbrooke railway station, early 1900s.

A view of the railway sidings at Pan Mill, 1920s. The sidings were used to house grain trucks which delivered to the mill.

This group is believed to be Newport railway staff, 1896.

		s. d.
To	Ashey – – – –	1/5
,,	Bembridge – – –	2/10
,,	Blackwater – – –	–/6
,,	Brading – – – –	2/4
,,	Calbourne – – –	1/3
,,	Carisbrooke Halt – –	–/4
,,	Cowes – – – –	1/–
,,	Freshwater – – –	2/5
,,	Godshill Halt – –	1/2
,,	Haven St. – – –	1/–
,,	Merstone – – –	} –/11
,,	Mill Hill – – –	
,,	Newchurch – – –	} 1/5
,,	Ningwood – – –	
,,	Ryde Esplanade – –	} 2/1
,,	,, Pier – – –	
,,	,, St. Johns Rd. – –	1/11
,,	St. Helens – – –	2/9
,,	St. Lawrence Halt – –	} 2/1
,,	Sandown – – –	
,,	Shanklin – – –	2/4
,,	Ventnor – – – –	2/5
,,	,, West – –	2/4
,,	Whippingham – –	–/6
,,	Whitwell – – –	1/8
,,	Wootton – – –	–/8
,,	Wroxall – – –	2/5

A list of rail fares from Newport as they were in 1948. It is interesting to note that at these prices 1s would cover the 5-mile journey from Newport to Cowes.

Coal barges wait to be unloaded at Newport Quay, 1909. Coal was used not only as fuel in the home, but also on the railways and for steam traction-engines on the road. Many such barges would also be unloaded at Cowes.

SECTION FOUR

Shops

With the advent of the motor cycle, many small businesses opened for the sole purpose of supplying motor-cycle accessories. These shops often included a full engineering service for the machines. Seen here in the early 1920s is Newport's Borough Hall motor-cycle shop, with concessionaire Stanley Russell (centre). The site is now occupied by Texas Homecare.

Upward's grocer's store in Pyle Street, 1920. It was demolished in 1963 and the site is now part of the Gateway complex.

Whittington the florist was situated in the High Street opposite the Castle Inn. The proprietor, Mr Whittington, is standing in the doorway, c. 1920.

Morris and Cowdery's shoe shop in the High Street. The site is now occupied by Boots the chemist. The wall here tells all!

Mrs Yelf poses in the doorway of her bakery and teashop, 1930s. This was situated in St James Square.

Moorman & Son was a furniture shop at Node Hill. Note the gas lamp over the door. The store is now the site of Sheath's petshop.

J.H. Williams' butcher's shop in the High Street. It was an open-fronted shop with iron shutters, and an interesting feature was a green fountain which worked during opening hours. On the closure of the business the fountain was moved to a Carisbrooke garden. The site is now occupied by W.H. Smith.

H.A. Pitcher's butcher's shop in Pyle Street is seen here dressed for Christmas, 1922.

Sheaf's Fishmarket in the High Street, 1930s. The shop was situated opposite Mill Street, and it is now a hairdresser's.

Coombes the saddlers in Node Hill, 1901. The man in the bowler hat is believed to be Mr Coombes, pictured with some of his staff.

Steel's Parkhurst grocery and confectionery store, c. 1930. This was situated in St James Street.

J.H. Linington the ironmonger sold everything from guns to tractors and tin tacks to steam engines. The shop was situated in St James Square, where the Nationwide Building Society now stands.

Edith Hampton, 1930. She is standing outside her doll shop in Node Hill.

Walter Neat (centre) stands outside his hardware shop, which is bedecked for the coronation of Edward VII, 1901. The shop was situated on the corner of Crocker Street and St James Street, and is now Margham's garage.

Walter Neat's horse-drawn delivery van, 1904. Note the wicker basket and tin bath hanging on the back.

This later photograph shows Walter Neat's ironmongery business. It became known as Neat Brothers in the 1920s.

Hornybrooke's cycle shop at Coppins Bridge, 1930s.

Mr Chiverton and his apprentice Gordon Hoskin stand outside the jeweller's shop in Pyle Street, early 1930s. The shop opened in 1927 and ten years later it moved to its present site in the High Street. It is still a thriving business.

Morris' furniture store in the High Street, at the turn of the century. Note how the furniture stands outside for all to examine.

'Ma' Freeman's was more of an 'eating house' than a café, as there was no menu. On offer was just the 'meal of the day', which included a sweet and a mug of tea. However, people would travel from all over the local area to have their dinner at Ma Freeman's. The two girls in front are Molly Freeman (with a hat) and Nancy O'Rourke.

To the left of Purkis the clothier's stood the hostelry nicknamed 'the Pig and Carrot'. Its real name was Piquet and Carouse – *Piquet* is a French card game and *carouse* is from the German *gar aus trinken* meaning roughly 'to drink in a merry fashion'. The hostelry was demolished many years ago.

Moody's was a greengrocer's and fruiterer's, although it obviously sold many other items. On Saturday evenings any fruit left would be taken home, made into jam and put on sale the next morning. This picture shows Harold Moody with his dog and delivery bike, 1930s.

Whitcher's clothier business stood on the corner of Holyrood Street and the High Street. It is pictured in the heavy snow of 1963. On the right stands Eric Gear, a bus driver.

Downer the newsagent's of Hunnyhill, 1930s.

Abraham's pork butcher's shop is seen here dressed for Christmas. It was once an extremely successful family concern, but it is now the site of Currys, in Node Hill.

This photograph, looking north, shows the old shops in Node Hill, early 1900s.

Another view of Node Hill, this time looking south. The shop on the right is Rugg's the tobacconist's.

The top of the town, with shop canopies pulled down, *c.* 1919. Also note the famous horse trough.

Dalby's shoe shop stood on the corner of Pyle Street and Node Hill. It is pictured in the 1890s.

King's grocer's shop stood next to the Eight Bells in Carisbrooke. Pictured here, 1934, is Mr King with his staff, including the bicycle delivery lad, Jim Davies.

Hayles' pork butcher's shop in St James Square, early 1920s. In front are the railings which were used to tie up beasts awaiting auction at the weekly market. The site is now part of Evans, the ladies' shop.

SECTION FIVE

Around the Town

Carisbrooke High Street, 1910.

Before . . . this photograph of South Street shows the houses and mews garages which were later demolished to make way for the new bus station.

After . . . a view of South Street in the 1960s, when the site had been cleared ready for the building work to commence.

Portland House Academy was a private school. It was situated on the corner of West Street and Trafalgar Road, and was run by Mr Barnes until its closure in 1928.

An early view of the Westminster stream, before the construction of the workshops and stores. Westminster Mill is in the centre.

Newport Almshouses in Crocker Street, 1910. They were refurbished in later years.

The Freemasons Tavern, on the corner of Lugley Street and St James Street. The pub closed in 1983, and the site is now a ladies' dress shop.

This is a rare picture of Newport Roller Rink, once situated on the corner of Lugley Street and Hearn Street. It was closed and demolished in the early 1930s.

Members of Newport Rowing Club return to the boathouse, 1901. The Ship and Launch Inn provides an appropriate background.

Canning Day's corner, early 1960s. This is now the site of Safeway's supermarket.

A Ford car lies on its side as a result of an accident outside Canning Day's, 1950s.

The rebuilding of Coppins Bridge viaduct, 1920s.

The junction of Castle Road and Whitepit Lane, 1885.

The Guildhall is seen here in the 1870s, before the clock tower was added.

This photograph is thought to be one of the earliest taken of the lower High Street. It dates from before 1870.

Shide Path, 1880s. This is now Medina Avenue.

A slightly later picture of Shide Path. Here, the railings have been added, changing Shide Path from a dirt lane to a roadway.

This photograph was taken a few minutes after the one on page 4, in the 1890s. The boy pushing a barrow has gone and a horse and trap have taken his place. Another horse and carriage (top) is entering the square from St James Street.

A postcard of St James Square, showing the sheep pens on market day, 1910.

This photograph of St James Square probably dates from October 1921.

St James Square, early 1900s.

Massey Harris binders are seen here on display for a sales promotion by J.H.
Linington's ironmonger's in St James Square, *c*. 1936.

St James Square, 1907. The Corn Exchange is on the extreme left.

The Savoy cinema, previously known as the Odeon, was built in 1938 at a cost of £10,000. It was demolished in 1984 and Dabells' furniture store now occupies the site.

This picture shows the original staff of the Odeon. On the left are Mr Newman, the manager, and Mr Reece, the commissionaire.

St James Square, 1894. The railings were used to tie up beasts awaiting auction on market day.

South Street, 1950.

The Guildhall is partially hidden by the heavy snows of 1881.

The High Street after the 1881 snowfalls.

The Trooper Inn in St James Street was noted for its very low ceilings. Seen here in 1958, it was demolished in the 1960s.

The Upper High Street, 1880s. Note the gravel road, which was later paved over in 1906 and eventually tarmacked in 1919.

The Lion Hotel in Carisbrooke, early 1900s.

Carisbrooke High Street, 1907. Leaning against the wall in the centre of the picture is a ladder used for mounting a four-in-hand stage coach.

The Falcon Inn and Barton the grocer's in Castle Road, early 1920s.

Carisbrooke Castle, 1921. On the extreme right is the governor's residence. The photograph was taken before the boom in tourism.

Coppins Bridge viaduct, 1890s. On the left is The Globe Inn and on the right is The White Lion.

Shide railway crossing is seen here closed to trains, 1924. Newport Golf Club is in the background.

Shide crossing, 1954. The platform and station buildings are behind.

With the advent of the railway and motor car many open spaces in the town were taken over, leaving just small pockets of natural habitat. One such pocket is the Lukely stream, under the railway viaduct at Hunnyhill, which has been home to many a swan.

The county council buildings and Seely Library, at the turn of the century. These were known as the Technical Institute and later became part of Node Hill School, which was owned by Reginald McKenna MP, President of the Board of Education. The first pupils were accepted in 1907.

Lacey's removal lorry from Bembridge waits in St Thomas' Square, Newport, 1932. The square was the collecting area for carriers. Seen here are Arthur Sprake, another haulier (left), Tom Lacey (centre) and his assistant, John Nightingale.

Pan Bridge is pictured in the heavy snows of 1963. On the right is Kate Chambers, a bus conductress.

Mrs Urry's Temperance Hotel in Pyle Street is seen here at the turn of the century.

The Brewery Bar in Trafalgar Road was later renamed the Globe and Laurel. It was demolished by Island Caravans and Trailers in 1986. A housing complex now stands on the site.

This photograph shows the funeral of Donald Biles, a local cattle dealer, who was killed by a bull, 1936. In front, with the umbrellas, are the Revd Mr MacKinnon and Mr Hamilton, the undertaker.

The Simeon Monument in Carisbrooke Road. The arches were erected for Queen Victoria's Golden Jubilee celebrations, 1887.

A rare view of the top of Hunnyhill, 1931.

The entrance to Fowler's Garage in Pyle Street, 1920s. Stan Williams (centre, with cap) became garage foreman in the early 1930s.

Simmonds' fish shop in Node Hill, 1922.

A First World War tank on display in Victoria Recreation Ground. This was eventually cut up in the 1940s to help the war effort.

Above, a line drawing of the original St Thomas' Church. Below, the dwellings in St Thomas' Square to the rear of the church. The building on the extreme left is God's Providence House. The drawings date from 1849.

SECTION SIX

Parades and Celebrations

The 1st Newport Scouts' band, known as The Old Guard, in St Thomas' Square, 1960s. Mike Squibb is the drum major.

A Scout jamboree, held in the grounds of Carisbrooke Castle, 1920s. The picture includes Lord Baden-Powell (centre right) and Lady Baden-Powell (seated, left).

This photograph shows Scouts assembled at the same jamboree.

Here, activities are taking place in the arena.

Spectators at the Carisbrooke Pageant held in Carisbrooke Castle grounds, 1907.

Children parade along the High Street before going into Castlehold Baptist Church, during the celebrations of the coronation of George V, 1910.

Children pass along Pyle Street for the coronation celebrations.

A parade of Scouts along the High Street, believed to be St George's Day in the 1920s.

Troops from Parkhurst Barracks march along Lower St James Street, probably on their way to Cowes for the funeral of Queen Victoria, 1901. They are seen here passing The Star Inn on the corner of Lugley Street. This inn burned down in 1910.

Funeral procession of Mayor Gilmartin, who died in office, 1908. The procession is passing the Crown and Sceptre, which was later destroyed in the blitz.

A crowd is gathered at a jumble sale in Newport, during the First World War. These sales were held at regular intervals to raise money for servicemen.

Armistice Day, 1918. A crowd awaits the official announcement and the arrival of the mayor and councillors, in St James Square.

An Armistice service in St Thomas' Square, 1921. It is attended by Princess Beatrice, who is sitting (top right) on a dais next to the Bishop of Winchester.

This photograph shows the inauguration of the cenotaph in St Thomas' Square, 1920.

Porchfield

Porchfield is a small village situated next to Newtown, which was once the island's capital, and lies approximately 4½ miles from Newport. One or two of its families have dominated the island's history, and the largest of these was the Mew family, who lived here from the early 1800s until the mid-1900s. This photograph shows their home, Porchfield Farmhouse, now known as Porchfield House.

In the 1800s, and until its closure in 1947, children from Porchfield and district attended Locks Green School. Here we see the schoolchildren dancing around the maypole, *c.* 1910.

The Mew family are seen here at harvest time, 1890.

The Mew family, 1905. Back row, left to right: Fred, Ethel, Ernest, Mary, Alan; front row: Winifred, Agnes, Edward, Caroline, Maurice, Lena.

The Mew girls are seen here in their teens, early 1900s. Left to right are Winifred, Agnes, Mary, Ethel and Lena.

Miss Gibson was a local personality who liveried her horse at the Mews' farm.

Caroline Mew feeds the chickens at Porchfield Farm, 1910.

A member of another prominent Porchfield family, Ted Holbrook, 1886.

One of the Mew boys sought work at Weeks' bakehouse in Trafalgar Road, Newport. He is among the bakers seen here standing behind the horse.

Another prominent Porchfield family were the Hawards. Seen here in 1872 are, left to right: Eliza, Caroline (who later married Edward Mew), Annie, Bessie.

A Porchfield Sunday School outing, early 1900s. The group includes Edward and Caroline Mew (standing, extreme right). Edward Mew was not only a farmer but was also the builder, undertaker, shopkeeper, local Methodist lay preacher and a Liberal councillor.

Acknowledgements

The writing and preparation of this book would not have happened had it not been for the help, advice, encouragement and cooperation of many people. Therefore I would like to thank the following:

Roy Brinton, Curator of the Carisbrooke Castle Museum
Mr and Mrs Aubrey Wray of Northwood • Phoebe Raddings of Yarmouth
Malcolm Johnson of Cowes • Bill Shepard of Newport • Reg Davies of
Newport • Ray Price of Hunnyhill Electrics, Newport • Mr Hamilton of
Newport • the Station Officer, Newport Fire Station • Bert Draper of Newport

And finally to Peter T.G. White, my friend and colleague, who assisted in the collation and the word processing of the letters and captions.